# The Wigmaker
# in Eighteenth-Century Williamsburg

**R**ICHARD GAMBLE, barber and peruke-maker of Williamsburg in the middle years of the eighteenth century, appears to have remained a bachelor all his life. Other than this he seems to have been no more improvident than the average craftsman of his time. That is to say, he came—or was brought—into court with startling frequency in an endless round of suits to collect unpaid debts.

He was in good company. Going to the law was part of the colonial way of life in Virginia, and everyone from a town's least citizen to the colony's greatest planter engaged in it. In fact, suing and being sued had some of the aspects of a game: the plaintiff in one case might shortly be defendant in another and witness in a third—and keep right on doing business with the other parties in all three cases!

Court records abound with evidence that Williamsburg wigmakers were just as impecunious and as contentious as any of the rest. Mr. Gamble, however, had an additional distinction—of a sort. While most debt cases reached settlement out of court or ended in judgment for the plaintiff, Gamble actually went to jail for debt. In the *Virginia Gazette* of May 8, 1752, appeared this announcement to the public:

BEING prevented carrying on my Business as usual by an Arrest for a Debt not justly my own. I hereby give Notice, That I have taken into Partnership with me *Edward Charlton*, late from *London*, who will carry on the Business, at my Shop, next Door to the *Raleigh* Tavern, in *Williamsburg*. Gentlemen, who please to favour us with their Orders for Wigs, &c. may depend on being well and expeditiously serv'd and oblige

Their very humble Servant<br>*Richard Gamble.*

*N. B.* All Persons who are indebted to me, are desired to pay the same to Mr. *Alexander Finnie*, who is properly impowered for that Perpose.

Alexander Finnie, co-defendant with Gamble in at least one large suit for debt—perhaps the one that led to Gamble's "Arrest"—was himself a wigmaker who had abandoned the craft for the arduous pleasures of innkeeping. He was proprietor at the time of the Raleigh Tavern, Williamsburg's largest and most famous hostelry.

When Gamble died, Edward Charlton, late from London, succeeded to the business and became in time Williamsburg's leading barber and wigmaker. His livelihood—as perhaps he foresaw—was already doomed when he retired from business shortly before the Revolution: the wig fashion was on the way out in England and would soon be dropped in America. And in any case his former clientele would vanish from the streets of Williamsburg when the capital of Virginia was moved to Richmond in 1780.

Charlton, Gamble, and Finnie were only three of some thirty men concerned with barbering and wigmaking in eighteenth-century Williamsburg. Once or twice between 1700 and 1780 the town apparently had to struggle along for short periods with but a single active practitioner of the craft. Usually there were at least two or three, and for a time in 1769 as many as eight plied their trade in the little capital city.

About some of these thirty or more men we know nothing today except their names. About others quite a few facts survive in one place or another, chiefly the records of the York County Court and the columns of the *Virginia Gazette*. In addition, Edward Charlton's account book of sales made and payments received during the years 1769 to about 1775 (there are some later entries) was found in the attic of a Williamsburg home only a few years ago. It helps immensely to round out our knowledge of his craft and clientele, and makes him almost inevitably the "representative" of his fellows in this account.

All of these Williamsburg barbers and perukemakers performed at least one, but not always all three, of the craft's

*Two customers and seven workers in an eighteenth-century French barber-wigmaker's shop. From left to right: a man (partly obscured in the shadow) prepares hair in the hackle; another sews weft to the peruke on the wig block in his lap; before the window a girl weaves strands of hair on the frame to make weft; a customer, standing, protects his face with a cloth as he dusts his head with powder; an apprentice shaves a second customer; in the background two workers heat curling irons in the fire; another apprentice dresses what appears to be a Ramillies wig on the stand.* DIDEROT basic services: (1) making, selling, and dressing wigs and false hair pieces for men and women; (2) cutting and dressing men's, women's, and children's natural hair; and (3) shaving men. Before we go into more detail on these aspects of the craft in colonial days, however, it may be well to peer briefly still further back into history.

## BEARDS, WIGS, AND HISTORY

The trouble with hair is that it persists in growing, and every once in a while something must be done about it. Over the millenia since time began—or at least since people began—that "something" has been manifold in variety: dyeing, bleaching, oiling, powdering, pomading, trimming, curling, straightening, shaving off completely, or augmenting with hair from horses, cows, goats, and from other human heads.

Shaving the face was not customary among the ancient Greeks until Alexander the Great ordered his soldiers to doff their beards lest the enemy use them as a convenient handle in close combat. Thereupon the Grecian tonsorial parlor, known as a *tonstrina*, added shaving to its previous services of trimming and dressing the hair and beard, massage, first aid, and minor surgery.

Roman barbers (the word comes from the Latin *barba* for beard) followed the example of their Greek colleagues when the beard passed out of favor during the Republic. The classic reply of the Roman general Archelaus rings true even today: asked by a talkative barber how he would like to be trimmed, Archelaus answered, according to Plutarch, "In silence."

From the onslaught of the barbarians (a word that comes not from *barba*, but from the Greek *barbaros*, meaning strange or rude) until about the thirteenth century, the craft of barbering probably reverted in most of Europe to its elementary procedures of trimming and dressing the hair and beard. In the latter century the first guilds of barbers were formed in both France and England, and by the seven-two articles used by wigmakers and the inventory of his estate listed none.

*George Lafong*—Kept shop in Williamsburg from 1762 to 1783, at one time selling a pair of curls to Patsy Custis, Washington's stepdaughter. Advertised on several occasions for a journeyman to help him, and in 1777 took Alexander Wiley into partnership. Nineteen years later Lafong turned up as a beggar on the streets of Norfolk.

*Walter Lennox*—First appeared in Williamsburg court records in 1759. From 1768 had his shop at the Sign of the Red Lion, where he also offered lodgings. His frequent advertisements for a journeyman indicate that he did a lively business. Lodged and boarded sick soldiers in the Revolution and supplied provisions to the army.

*Robert Lyon*—In various businesses from 1749 to 1771, first as barber and wigmaker. Took up tavernkeeping at the Sign of Edinburgh Castle, near the Capitol, in 1755. Four years later had become a merchant, whose store faced on Market Square.

*Alexander Maitland*—With his partner, John Bryan, advertised wigmaking services once in 1752. Thereafter Maitland appears to have moved to Yorktown.

*James Martin*—Court records and the like show him to have been in Williamsburg from 1760 to 1766; he never advertised in the *Virginia Gazette*. At his death he left a large estate including 18 wigs and other barbering articles as well as items that point strongly to his being also a tavernkeeper.

*James Nichols*—Coming from London, he opened shop first in Petersburg in 1772 and three years later in Williamsburg. Took Richard Charlton into a brief and unsuccessful partnership in 1776. Advertised his property

Pepys's final word on the subject was to wonder "what will be the fashion after the plague is done, as to periwiggs, for nobody will dare to buy any haire, for fear of the infection, that it had been cut off the heads of people dead of the plague." He need not have been concerned on that score; the fashion throve better after the plague than before, attaining its greatest development under Queen Anne, when the long curls of men's full-bottomed wigs covered the back and shoulders and floated down over the chest. In France, according to Diderot's *Encyclopedia* (published 1751–1772), late seventeenth-century *perruques* were so long and so much adorned that they commonly weighed as much as two pounds and cost more than 1,000 *ecus* (silver coins about the size of a dollar).

Milady's hairdress reached even more preposterous extremes in the many-tiered and bejewelled "fontanges" of Louis XIV's court (an exaggeration he disapproved in vain) about 1700. After a period of some moderation the style reappeared in the yard-high "heads" dictated to fashion by Marie Antoinette before she lost hers. If English and colonial women did not go to the extreme, they nevertheless followed the style. A letter to the New York *Journal or General Advertiser* in 1767 complained that "it is now the Mode to make the Lady's Head of twice the natural Size, by means of artificial Pads, Boulsters, or Rolls" which —the writer had on good authority—came from hospital patients dead of the smallpox and of "a Distemper still more disagreeable."

## WIG SHOPS IN WILLIAMSBURG

The shop that Richard Gamble entrusted to his new partner in 1752 stood next door to the Raleigh Tavern, in what was sometimes called "the most public part of the city." Certainly no better location in Williamsburg could have been found for a barber shop than on the Duke of Gloucester Street in the block nearest the Capitol.

*"The Preposterous Head Dress, or the Feathered Lady"* is the title of this satirical print issued in London in 1776. Contemporary accounts indicate that the artist did not greatly exaggerate either the size or the composition of the headdresses affected by fashionable ladies in the capitals of Europe. Colonial women seem not to have dressed their hair in such heights of fashion.

The broad main street of Williamsburg, muddy or dusty as the season decreed, stretched westward from the Capitol nearly a mile to the College of William and Mary. During most of the year it saw only the normal activity of a small colonial town. But several times each year—when the courts and perhaps the Assembly met—the town's population doubled or tripled. These "Publick Times" were almost field days of litigation, commercial negotiation, and merrymaking. Then it was that innkeepers and craftsmen lucky enough to have located in that first block knew how fortunate they were.

One small shop also near the Raleigh had been a barbering and wigmaking establishment at least since John Peter Wagnon bought it in 1734. It remained so through the long ownership of Wagnon's one-time apprentice, Andrew Anderson, and the short occupancy of two successor barbers and wigmakers, William Peake of Yorktown and James Currie. Across the street from the Raleigh had stood the shop of Jean Pasteur, one of Williamsburg's first known wigmakers. Somewhere nearby Alexander Finnie made wigs before moving to the Raleigh itself, and Anthony Geohegan did so later—perhaps in the same shop.

A little farther uptown William Peake had briefly set up business as a barber in Mr. Dunn's Crown Tavern, opposite the printing office. James Nichols first opened his shop in "the corner room of the brick house where Mrs. Singleton lives"—now better known as the Brick House Tavern. And somewhere along the same crowded street Richard Charlton (who was somehow related to Edward and had at least a passing acquaintance with wigmaking) kept his well-patronized tavern.

Other craftsmen also located in the same neighborhood. Not far beyond the Raleigh hung the sign of James Craig's jewelry, watch, and silversmith shop, the Golden Ball. And next to it was the millinery store of the sisters Margaret and Jane Hunter—the latter of whom married her neighbor Edward Charlton.

*The restored shop of the barber and perukemaker in Williamsburg. It stands on Duke of Gloucester Street next to the King's Arms Tavern and across from the Raleigh Tavern. In dimensions, appearance, and equipment it is believed to resemble quite closely a shop that stood on the site about 1770 and may have been occupied successively by the partnerships of Geohegan and Brazier and of Charlton and Nichols.*

The size of Edward Charlton's barber and wig shop is now unknown. For some time it was probably no larger than a front room of the house he owned opposite the Raleigh. Andrew Anderson's shop was in a building sixteen feet square. The barber shop next to the King's Arms Tavern is shown on later insurance papers to have been sixteen by twenty feet—and these are the approximate dimensions of the restored barber and perukemakers's shop.

## MASTERS, SERVANTS, AND MATERIALS

In such a small shop it seems unlikely that even a leading wigmaker could have had very many helpers. But Edward Charlton at one time had four apprentices and journeymen, and one of his contemporaries, Robert Lyon, in the space of two years had five known bond servants, at least three identified as barber-wigmakers.

Apprenticeship to a master barber and perukemaker was the normal—in fact the only—way for a boy to learn the trade. The Williamsburg wigmakers presumably all entered the craft in this manner, though Andrew Anderson is the only one about whom the record is clear. Presumably, too, most of them had apprentices in turn; but here the surviving information is quite skimpy.

Journeymen (craftsmen who had finished their apprentice training but had not yet gone into business as their own masters) were in good demand and apparently in good supply. Alexander Finnie gave notice in a 1745 issue of the *Virginia Gazette* that he was "in want of Two or Three

Journeymen, that understand the Business of a Barber and Peruke-maker," and promised any who applied "good Encouragement." The response to this ad was prompt, for the very next issue of the *Gazette* contained this notice by the master barber and wigmaker whose shop was directly across the street from Finnie's:

> *Whereas my honest Neighbour, that has advertis'd for Two or Three Journeymen, has lately seduced One from my Service, in a clandestine and undermining Manner; which I am well persuaded, that no Man but one of his Principles would have done: Therefore it's to be hoped, that one of the Number he has advertised for, will come into my Service, in Lieu of him who has been so villanously cajol'd as above, who may depend on having good Encouragement, from*

> Andrew Anderson.

Whether Anderson lured anyone into his employ by this ad does not appear. But Finnie a year later announced that he had just imported from London a shipment of wigmaking materials and also "some exceeding good Workmen." With what has the ring of smug satisfaction he concluded: "As I have a great many good Workmen, Gentlemen and others may depend on being speedily and faithfully served, in the best Manner."

Finnie's mention of imported materials was typical. Time and again the announcements of Williamsburg wigmakers contain phrases such as "Just arrived, a choice Parcel of Hairs, prepared by the best Hands in London," or "A Fresh Cargoe of live human Hairs, already curl'd and well prepared." By far the larger portion of hair used in Williamsburg-made wigs was imported from England, either by the perukemaker himself or by colonial hair merchants.

According to Diderot's *Encyclopedia*, hair from regions such as Flanders, where beer and cider were the common beverages, made superior wigs; women's hair was better than men's; country women's better than city women's; and chestnut was the most desirable color—except that white wigs should be made of hair that once had been black. Furthermore, avowed the same authority, "In general the hair of persons not given to excesses lasts a long time, while that of men who live in sexual debauchery, or of women who give themselves to the uses of men, has less sap, dries out, and loses its quality."

If colonial wigmakers were aware of this dictum—which seems unlikely—they paid it no attention, buying hair from abroad with never a query as to the personal habits of the original wearers, and showing similar indifference in purchasing local locks:

> THE subscriber proposes purchasing HAIR for WIGS, and hopes he will soon be able to supply wigmakers with that article, of different kinds. He is in want of a quantity of human hair, both long and short, of any colour, for which he will give one shilling *per* ounce, or more, according to the quality. Apply to Mr. *James Nichols*, barber in *Williamsburg*, who will receive it and pay the money, or to me in *Petersburg*.
>
> GEORGE LONG.

## COLONIAL CLIENTELE

A few of the Williamsburg barbers and perukemakers advertised their readiness to dress ladies' hair, and Charlton regularly made "curls" for his customers' wives. But most seem to have confined themselves wholly—or almost so—to barbering and bewigging male clients.

These clients were either town dwellers or members of the plantation gentry, who were the colony's economic, political, and social elite. Of every hundred Virginians, eighty or more were small farmers or farm workers and did not own wigs. Devereaux Jarratt, the son of a poor but industrious farmer near Williamsburg, recalled later in life in his memoirs:

> A *periwig*, in those days, was a distinguishing badge

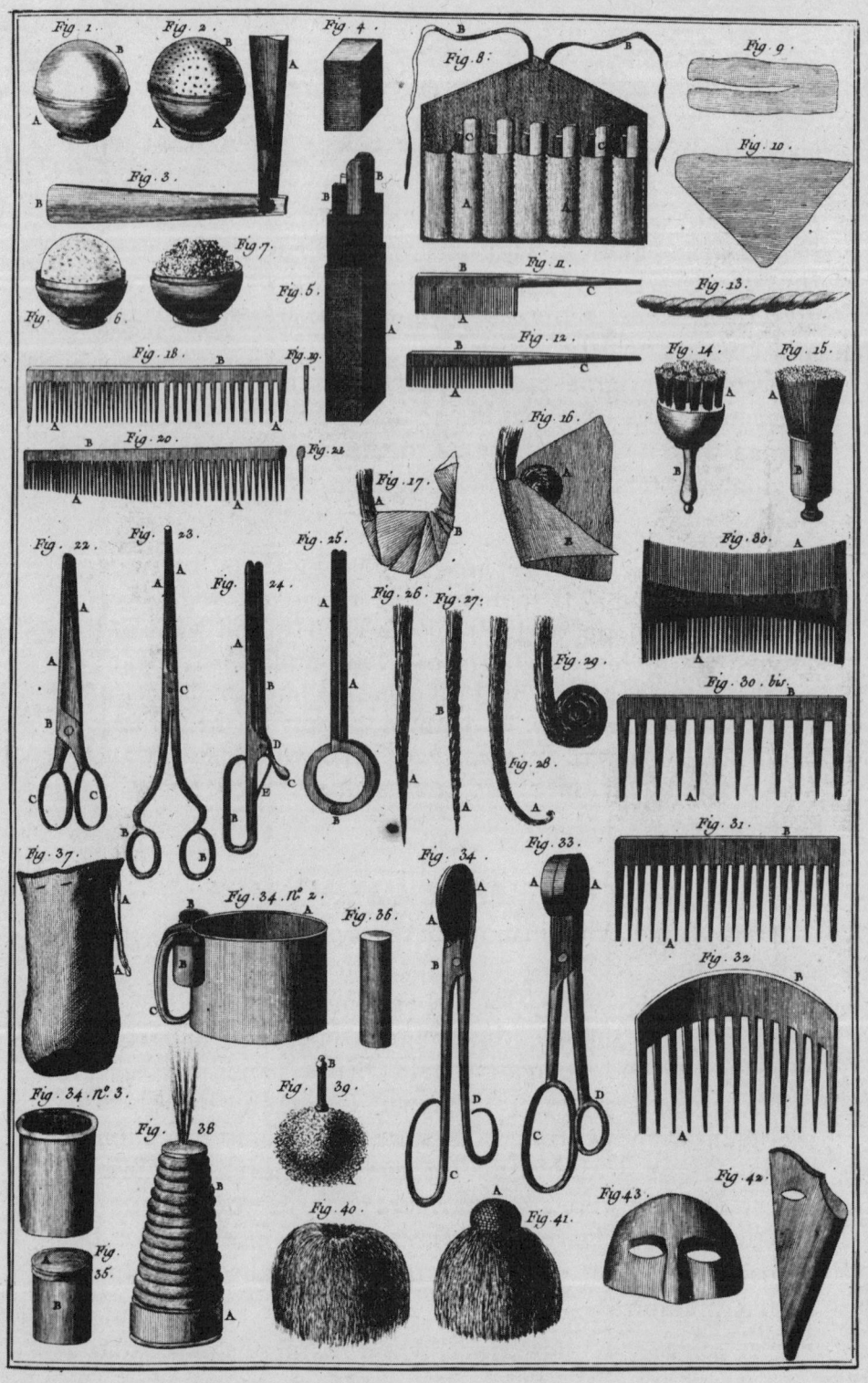

Some of the tools and equipment of the barber-wigmaker, especially those used for shaving and hair dressing. Note in particular the powdering masks in the lower right corner that covered the faces of customers while their hair or wigs were being dusted with powder. DIDEROT of *gentle folk*—and when I saw a man riding the road, near our house, with a wig on, it would so alarm my fears, and give me such a disagreeable feeling, that, I dare say, I would run off, as for my life.

And an anonymous traveler of the 1740s observed that in Maryland:

'Tis an odd Sight, that except some of the very elevated Sort, few Persons wear Perukes, so that you would imagine they were all sick, or going to bed: Common People wear Woollen and Yarn Caps; but the better ones wear white Holland or Cotton: Thus they travel fifty Miles from Home. It may be cooler, for ought I know; but, methinks, 'tis very ridiculous.

Perhaps on the frontier men allowed their beards to go unshorn. In the settled areas and towns, however, only a clean-shaven face was acceptable to the fashion that simultaneously demanded false hair on the head. Most men probably shaved themselves, and some, like Councillor Robert Carter and Dr. John Sequeira, had slaves trained to do their barbering. Of the rest a goodly number visited Charlton's shop almost daily and paid him an annual fee for "shaving and dressing." We do not know if this meant shaving the face or the head or both; "dressing," of course, normally referred to care of the wig.

Some among Charlton's regular customers for shaving and dressing, however, never bought a wig from him. Either they imported their own directly from a maker like Thomas Clendinning of Glasgow, or else they wore no wig. To defy fashion in this second manner must have taken some courage, for the wig was an important badge of social rank, particularly among the upper and would-be upper classes.

But it was not an infallible one. Negro slaves may sometimes have been decked out in white wigs: those who were the liveried house slaves, coachmen, and the like, of the ostentatiously rich planters. On the other hand, such a well-to-do and fashion-conscious man as George Washington seems from portraits and other records to have worn no wig at all, though he kept his own hair well powdered and curled. In the lesser ranks craftsmen, indentured servants, and apprentices sometimes did and sometimes did not wear wigs.

Washington, who often lodged when in Williamsburg at the tavern of Richard Charlton, was not among Edward Charlton's customers for any barbering service. Peyton Randolph, however, the speaker of the House of Burgesses, was an excellent patron. He bought two brown dress bob wigs every year, and each December paid for a year's shaving and dressing. John Randolph, the attorney general, was another regular customer, who paid nothing for several years, then settled his large bill partly in "cash," partly by "the pardon of a Negro," and partly with some horses.

The cash receipts that Charlton entered in his accounts may in rare instances have included clinking money. But the colonies were forbidden to mint their own, and coin of the realm was exceedingly scarce. So Charlton's income was largely paper currency of one kind or another: perhaps Virginia currency printed by William Hunter at the printing office on Duke of Gloucester Street years before; perhaps bills of exchange on a London merchant; most likely warehouse receipts for varying amounts of stored tobacco— these being a form of legal tender universally acceptable in the tobacco colonies.

Robert Carter Nicholas, treasurer of the colony, Thomas Everard, mayor of Williamsburg, George Mason of Gunston Hall, author of the Virginia Declaration of Rights, George Wythe, professor of law at the College, and Wythe's former student, the youthful Thomas Jefferson, all visited Charlton's shop more or less faithfully. Jefferson, experimenting as usual, first bought a brown dress queue wig and then a brown tie wig before he settled on the brown dress bob that was the prevailing style.

Another of Charlton's famous patrons, "Mr Patrick Hanrey Esqʳᵉ," bought only one peruke of him in the half-dozen years of the account book. He brought it back once

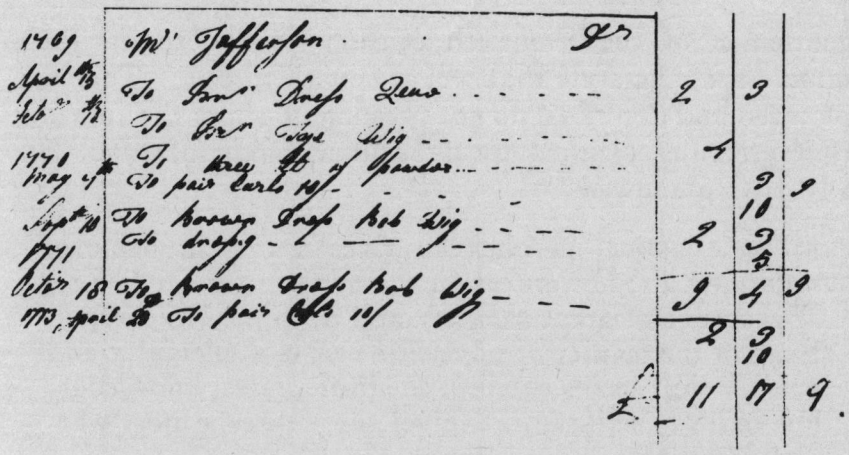

*Part of a page from Edward Charlton's account book, showing purchases by Thomas Jefferson of four wigs, two pairs of curls, three pounds of powder, and one dressing during the years 1769 (when he came to his first session as a member of the House of Burgesses), 1770, 1771, and 1773. Jefferson spent most of 1772, the year of his marriage, at Monticello, letting public business and Williamsburg get along without him.*

for alteration, but never for dressing. Perhaps this was the brown wig that one contemporary remembered "exhibited no indication of great care in the dressing." Another acquaintance recalled, however, that "at the bar of the General Court, [Henry] always appeared in full suit of black cloth or velvet, and a tye wig, which was dressed and powdered in the highest style."

Among the shop's other patrons were innkeepers, blacksmiths, a saddler, a silversmith, printers, clergymen, physicians—indeed, from wealthy planters like Robert Carter, Ralph Wormeley, and John Page to such unglamorous persons as Humphrey Harwood, plasterer and brick mason, Charlton made wigs for them all.

## THE MOST POPULAR PERUKES

The French *Encyclopédie Perruquière* listed 45 styles of wig in its 1727 edition, 115 styles in that of 1764. While a complete catalogue is impossible here, some description in words and pictures of the most frequent varieties may assist gentlemen of the twentieth century to choose (in their mind's eye) the style that would suit them best. The wigs pictured and described do not presume to share the amazing characteristics claimed by a London maker of 1760. His advertising avowed:

> to ecclesiastical perukes he gives a certain demure, sanctified air; he confers on the tye-wigs of the law an appearance of great sagacity and deep penetration; on those of the faculty of physick he casts a solemnity and gravity that seems equal to the profoundest knowledge. His military smarts . . . [give] the wearer a most war-like fierceness.

As for color, any style might be made up in any of the several colors favored for wigs: black, white, grizzle (an iron-gray mixture of black and white hair), brown, and flaxen are mentioned most often in surviving accounts. Less popular shades included milk white, light natural, yellowish, pale, chestnut, auburn, piss-burnt, and gray. Red was deemed a "disagreeable colour" for hair and was rarely if ever used in wigs.

The styles here shown were all popular at some time during the eighteenth century, though perhaps some of them were worn more often in England and France than in the colonies. On the other hand, a popular colonial style, the "Albemarle" wig, is not in our catalogue because nothing has been found to tell what it looked like.

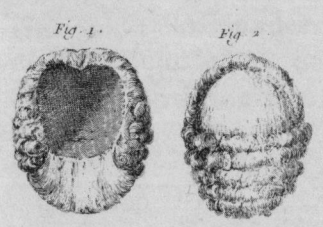

No eighteenth-century illustration of a bob wig, so labeled, has been found. This picture, from Diderot's *Encyclopedia* (like all the others in this group) shows a "bonnet" or "short wig." The brown dress bob favored by so many of Edward Charlton's customers must have been very similar. A plain bob presumably had fewer curls, but neither it nor the dress bob would have had any queue or hanging side curls.

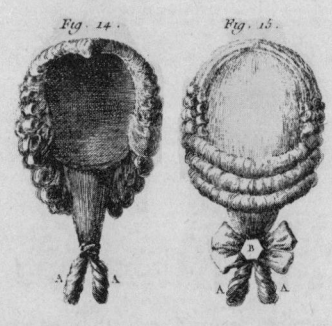

This "brigadier wig" shows what a few of Charlton's patrons ordered from him. It was known also as a major wig and a military wig. The "tye wig" mentioned in Charlton's accounts must have looked very much like this (again we lack any clear contemporary illustration) except that it had more than two curls tied at the nape of the neck.

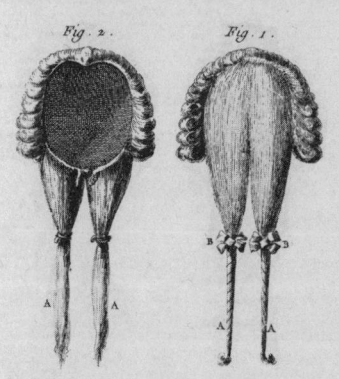

What Charlton called a "queue wig" might have been any wig with a tail—or even with two, like this double pigtail. The tails were usually bound tightly with black ribbon, though sailors used leather. A single queue, braided but not bound, with a large bow at the top and a small bow at the bottom, was known as a "Ramillies wig" after the battle at that place (1706). The wearer of a Ramillies often doubled the end of the queue back up to the wig and held it with a comb or ribbon.

In the "bag wig" the long hair at the back was simply tied inside a black taffeta bag, usually with a rosette of black ribbon for decoration. In England and France this style, like so many others, was carried to such an extreme that the bag eventually covered the wearer's entire shoulders. The exaggeration at least had the virtue of protecting his clothing from the pomade and powder of the wig. It was going out of fashion in Virginia by Charlton's time. Note the small strap and buckle on the wig.

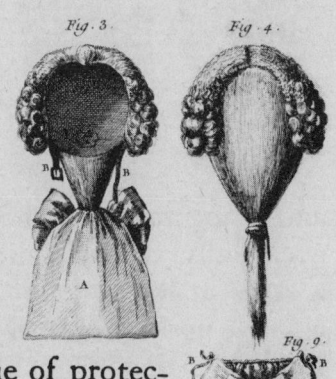

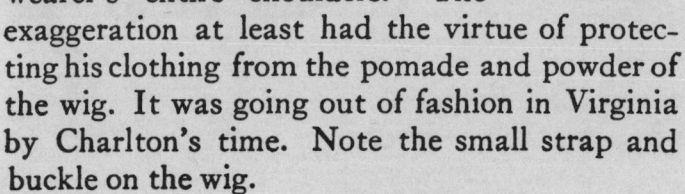

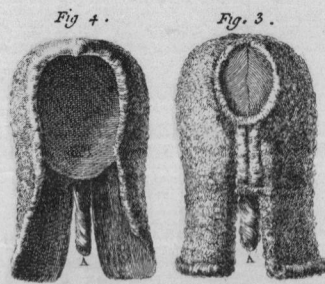

*Fig 4.    Fig. 3.*

By the time of Diderot's *Encyclopedia*, the "square wigs" shown here were the nearest remnants of the full-bottomed wigs that had gone out of style about 1740. These last can still be seen, however, in portraits of royalty and nobility of the seventeenth century and early years of the eighteenth, and of course the style still holds for English judges when they are on the bench.

This, incredibly, was called a "natural wig," and was supposed to resemble the wearer's own hair. It fell down behind in long, straight locks, ending either with a single roll, or tapering away into a series of ringlets.

The resemblance between this "knotted wig" and its distant predecessor, the full-bottomed wig,

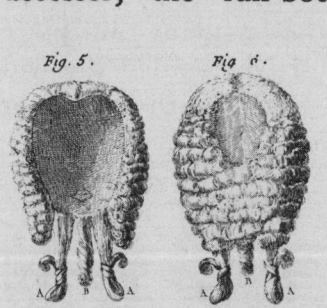

*Fig. 5.    Fig 6.*

may not be apparent at first glance. The flowing locks of the full-bottomed and campaign wigs (the latter having two long curls falling to the front of each shoulder) were inconvenient to travelers, sportsmen, and soldiers. So they adopted the habit of knotting up the curls on both sides and tying together those in back; eventually this expedient became a style in its own right, but with a single corkscrew curl in back.

The "cadogan" or "club wig," its name attributed to the first Earl of Cadogan, became popular in England in the 1770s,

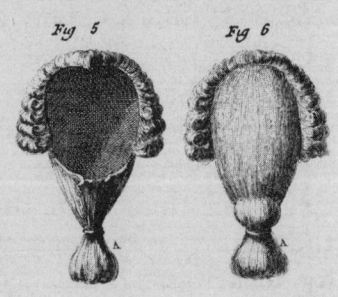

*Fig 5    Fig 6*

especially with the foppish young men who called themselves "Macaronis" and went to absurd extremes in style,
wearing cadogans several times the size of this modest
example.  The queue of straight hair was looped back on
itself and tied with string or ribbon to form a vertical bow
of hair.

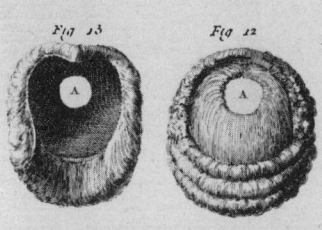

This is the kind of clerical wig,
with built-in tonsure, that Roman
Catholic clergy in France wore. Anglican clerics in Virginia, as Charlton's accounts testify, wore brown
dress bobs just like those of so
many of their parishoners.

## THE MAKING OF A WIG

The eighteenth-century wig was built up of rows of hair
woven at the root ends to cross-threads, each row being
then sewn to a net-and-ribbon skullcap or "caul."  The
steps in making a queue wig would differ, of course, in some
detail from those in making a wig without a queue.  But
the basic procedures in the eighteenth-century manner of
perukemaking are the same for any style, and can be set
forth briefly under the following seven headings:

(1) *Taking the Measurements*—The customer's head (pref-
erably shaved) is measured with a strip of paper about an
inch wide, each measurement being recorded by a scissor-
nick in the edge of the strip.  There are five essential dimensions to take: (a) from the top center of the forehead over
the head to the nape of the neck; (b) from one temple to the
other around the back of the head; (c) over the top of the
head from ear to ear (to the top of the ears for a wig "with
ears," i.e., with ears showing, to the middle of the ears for a
half-eared wig, and to the bottom of the ears for a full-
bottomed wig); (d) from the middle of either cheek to the
back of the head; and (e) from the top center of the forehead to either temple.

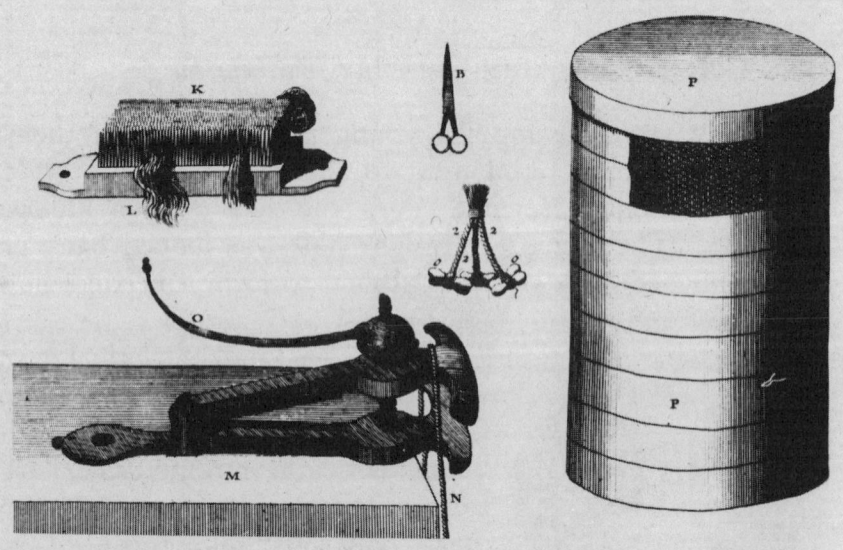

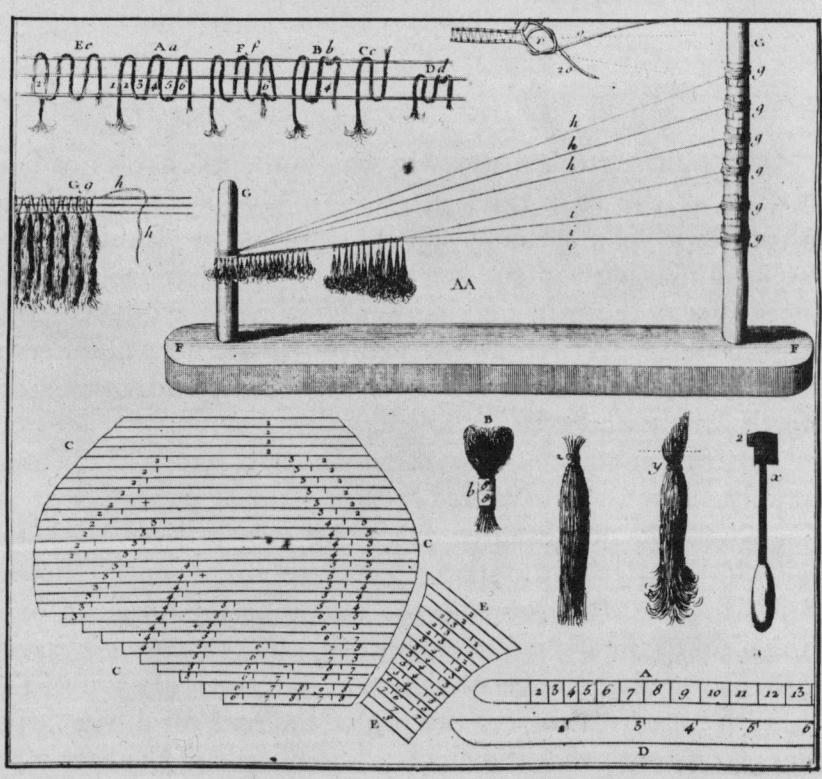

*The illustrations on this page come from François-Alexandre-Pierre de Garsault's* **The Art of the Wigmaker,** *published in France in 1767. At the top is a hackle, with two parcels of hair being combed through it. Next are shears, curling pins, and a cylindrical oven for heating and drying curls. The instrument below the hackle is a wigmaker's vise attached to a table top. Most prominent in the lower picture is the six-thread weaving frame, with hair strands of two different lengths tied to the lower threads. Above it and to the left are the various knots employed. The odd-shaped pattern at the lower left with each parallel line bearing several numbers produced a wig to fit the head of some eighteenth-century gentleman.*

(2) *Preparing the Hair*—Before it can be used in wig-making, hair must be cleaned, arranged according to length, quality, and color, and curled. Tied in small parcels, the hair is cleaned by thorough powdering with fine sand or mill dust from a flour mill; this absorbs the oil and grease from the hair and is then shaken out. Next the hair is combed or carded through a "hackle" and separated into parcels of different lengths. The wigmaker's vise, fixed to the table top in a horizontal position, holds each parcel of hair in turn (by the root ends) while the craftsman rolls the hair—in a curl-paper—onto curling pins made of pipe clay. These rolls he boils for three hours and then partially dries in a small charcoal oven. The loaded curlers are then piled up, taken to the bakery, covered with a shell of rye dough, and baked in a moderate oven. When the loaf is returned to the wig shop and broken open, the curls will have absorbed some moisture from the dough and must again be dried out in the charcoal oven. Finally dried and cooled, the curled hair can be taken off the pins and combed out in the hackle, further separated by lengths if necessary, and the root ends of each parcel trimmed off evenly. If the hair is thin and needs to be filled out with horsehair, or if hair of different colors is to be mixed to achieve a desired shade, this is the time to do it.

(3) *Making the Pattern*—The wigmaker's pattern is a weaving pattern; it shows how many rows of hair will be needed in a wig of the customer's size, how long each row must be, and how long the hair in each part of each row must be in order to make a wig of the desired style. On a piece of squared paper the wigmaker draws as many parallel lines as his measurements of the customer's head tell him are needed. Each successive line will be longer or shorter, also, as may be necessary to fit the customer's head. On each line—or portion of a line—he marks the length of hair he will use in that part of the wig. In determining this the wigmaker relies partly on his own experience, partly on pattern books or similar sources.

(4) *Weaving the Hair*—The rows of hair are woven on a simple frame of two upright posts holding three (or six) silk threads stretched tight. The wigmaker takes several strands of hair by the root ends and weaves them around the silk warp threads, using one of a number of possible weaves. He continues weaving a few strands at a time, sliding the woven strands tight together until he has a strip of weft as long as the pattern calls for. He winds the finished strip onto one post as more thread unwinds from the other, and does another row. If the frame holds six threads, the lower three are used for the right side of the wig (with the curl of the hair toward the weaver) and the upper three for the left side (with the hair curling away from the weaver).

(5) *Mounting the Caul*—From his assortment of hollowed out elm or ash wig blocks of different sizes and shapes the wigmaker selects the one that corresponds to the customer's head measurements. On it he outlines the proposed wig in inch-wide "mounting ribbon" of silk, carefully measuring, stretching, folding, and lightly tacking as he goes. Then he fixes the ribbon firmly in place with strong thread stretched around two rows of small nails, called "wig points," one row on either side of the ribbon. Next he sews a fine net of cotton or silk to the mounting ribbon all around, with appropriate folds and tucks to fit the curvature of the wig block, and trims off the excess. He then adds two strips of "covering ribbon" three and a half inches wide across the top of the wig, one from front to back, the other from side to side, basting them to the net and sewing them firmly to the mounting ribbon. He may add a drawstring or even a small strap and buckle at the back so the wearer can keep his wig on tighter.

(6) *Sewing the Strips of Weft to the Caul*—Following his pattern for length of rows and length of hair, the wigmaker now sews to the caul the strips of weft he has previously woven, using a simple straight stitch. Except for the rows framing the face, which start at the front edge and go

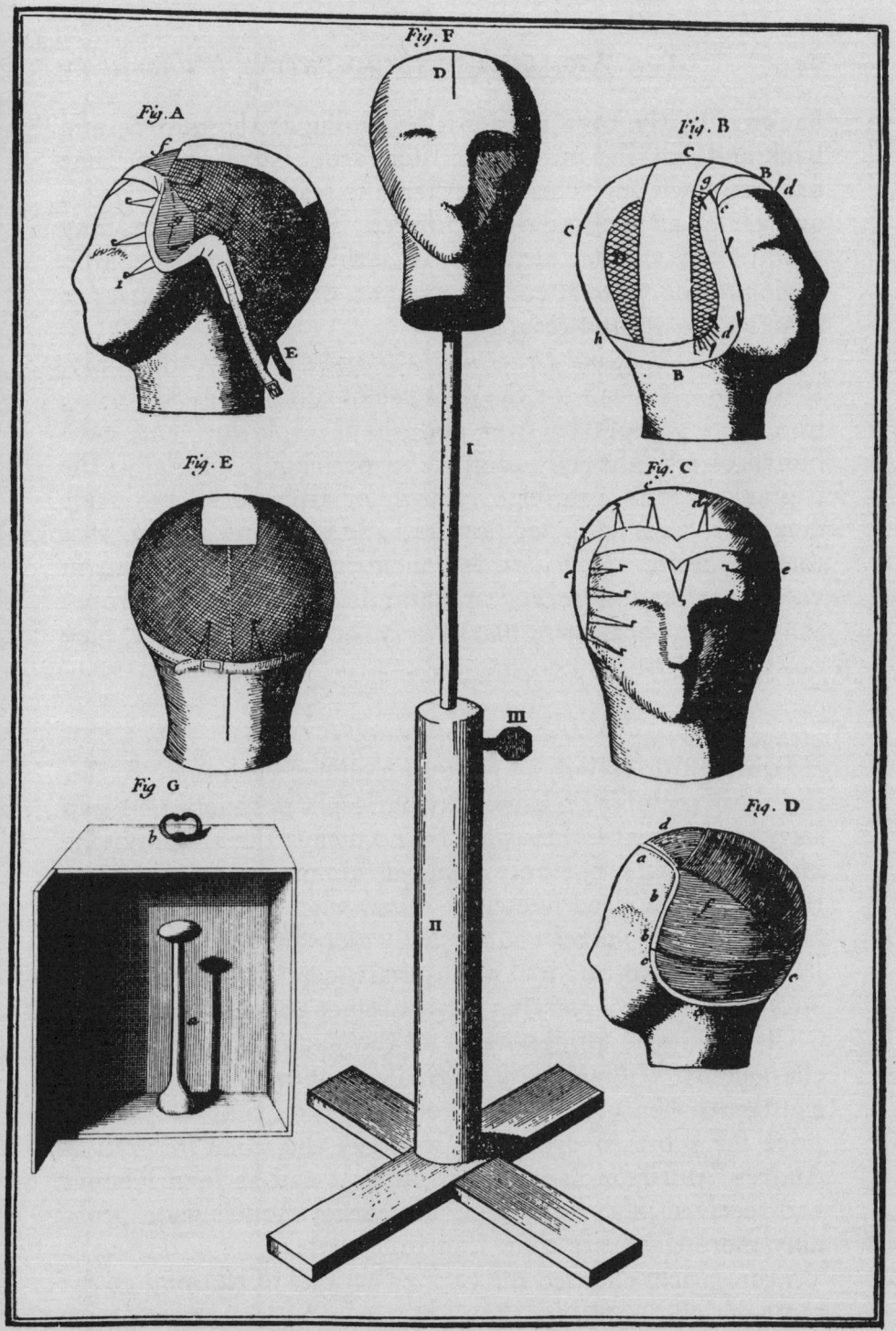

*Here are a group of wig blocks, one on an adjustable stand for easy pinning of the caul, the others with cauls in various stages of completion. Wigs not in use at the time or being taken on the owner's travels were kept or carried in wig boxes like that shown.* GARSAULT backwards, the rows are sewn beginning at the bottom and back and working upward and forward.  Rows of short fine hair are sewn very close together, the rest in parallel rows a quarter of an inch apart.  Different styles, of course, may require a particular sequence of sewing the proper combination of short, long, curled, straight, or horsehair tresses to achieve the desired result.

(7) *Finishing and Dressing the Wig*—As the words imply, these processes call for the deft use of comb, fingers, curling iron, and scissors to trim and shape each curl and each bunch of straight hair to graceful perfection.  Finally, the wigmaker adds a rosette, a bag, or ribbons as the style demands, and pomade, powder, and perfume to the customer's desire.  The powder, incidentally, may be had in various colors and serves to maintain the wig in the proper shade or tint of brown, black, gray, or white.  In fact, blue powder was not unknown.

## STYLES AND PRICES

If brown dress bob wigs at 43 shillings each were by far the most popular of Edward Charlton's products—he sold sixty in one year—they were by no means the only style he made.  Perukes not only came in almost endless variety; their prices differed likewise.  Even wigs of the same style from the same maker could vary widely in price (according to the kind and quality of materials, care in workmanship, etc.) as the accompanying advertisement shows.

Clendinning's prices were in the same range as those charged by Williamsburg wigmakers through most of the eighteenth century.  It is worth remark that Charlton's price for a brown dress bob wig was the same in 1770 as Andrew Anderson had charged in 1752 and as Jean Pasteur had received in 1726, though the earlier models were probably more elaborate than Charlton made.

From prices charged for various articles of clothing at the same period, it appears that a man could outfit himself with hat, coat, shirt, breeches, hose, and shoes for about what

# THOMAS CLENDINNING,

## WIG-MAKER, in *GLASGOW,*

UNDERTAKES to furnish all the GENTLEMEN in *Virginia,* that are pleased to favour him with their Commands, in WIGS of *all Sorts and Fashions,* at the Prices under-mentioned, according to the Goodness and Size ; in which Particular he promises to restrict himself to the lowest Rates he charges any of his Customers living in *Glasgow.*

HE is always possess'd of a large Stock of the *best HAIRS of all Colours*; and, as he proposes to keep the *best Workmen* in his *Employ,* and to regulate his *Fashions* by the *present Mode* at *LONDON,* he makes no Doubt of giving *entire Satisfaction* both in the *Goodness* and *Cheapness* of his WORK, which will be considerably under the *London* Prices.

Fair *Bob Wigs,* from 30 *sh.* to 3 *l.*
*Grizled Brigadier Wigs* and *Roses,* from 14 *sh.* to 30 *sh.*
*Grizled Spencer Wigs* and *Roses,* from 14 *sh.* to 25 *sh.*
*Grizled Bobs, Long* and *Short,* from 14 *sh.* to 30 *sh.*
*Brown Brigadier* and *Spencer Wigs,* from 10 *sh.* 6 *d.* to 16 *sh.* 6 *d.*
*Black Bobbs* and *Black Naturals,* from 8 *sh.* to 12 *sh.*
*Pale* and *Brown Bobs,* of the best Kinds, from 8 *sh.* to 12 *sh.*
And all *Sorts* for BOYS.

THE Method he would propose to take in answering his *Commissions,* is as follows :

" THAT the Gentlemen forward their Orders to himself, or to any of
" their Friends in *Glasgow,* expressing the Colour, Fashion of the Wigs,
" and Dimensions of the Caul, and the Price about which they would have
" the Wigs made up.

" OR, if they lodge a *Memorandum,* as above-mentioned, at the *Raw-*
" *leigh* Tavern in *Williamsburg,* several Copies of the same will be for-
" warded to him by different Opportunities, and he will immediately, upon
" Receipt thereof, have the Wigs wrought up agreeable to the Directions,
" and sent to *Virginia* by the first Ship that offers, directed to the same
" House, where they may be called for.

" UPON Delivery of the Wigs, the first-cost Price to be paid at the
" current Exchange, together with the common Premium of Insurance, and
" Six Pence a-Pound, as Commission, for the Trouble of receiving and de-
" livering the Wigs, and remitting the Money from *Virginia.*

" HE will charge nothing for the Boxes nor Freight : And, if the Wigs
" do not please at Sight, the Gentlemen are not bound to take them.

" EACH Gentleman's Name shall be mark'd upon the Wigs ; and along
" with each Box there will be sent an Invoice of the Whole, distinguishing
" the several Commissions, and including Insurance.

" AND, that the Gentlemen may be the better satisfied that Justice is
" done them in the Prices, *&c.* the Wigs will be examined, and the In-
" voice attested by Mr. *RICHARD OSWALD* Junior, Merchant
" in *Glasgow.*"

At Glasgow *the* 25*th* February, 1744-5.

### THOMAS CLENDINNINO.

*This advertisement is dated "At Glasgow the 25th February, 1744-5." It actually appeared in the Virginia Gazette of June 6, 1745, more than three months after Thomas Clendinning penned it. With transatlantic postal service so slow, the mail-order business that Clendinning solicited must have been less than rushing. It appears that he did not advertise in the Virginia Gazette again.*

his wig would cost him. Put another way, a suitably cheap wig might easily cost a journeyman his wages for two to three weeks, while a wealthy planter might pay nearly as much for one "Grisell Tye Wig" as a servant's board cost for a year.

Charlton's account book shows that shaving and dressing also came at different prices according to the services given. The charge for a year usually amounted to two pounds three shillings. It might, however, be as little as the one pound five shillings that Peter Pelham twice incurred or as much as the four pounds that Speaker Randolph paid. Pelham, organist at Bruton Parish Church and keeper of the colony's gaol, found time in a busy life to father a family of sixteen children but never got around to paying his little debt to the barber. The account book shows it, along with 13 years' accrued interest, still unpaid in 1784.

Besides the 60 brown dress bobs he made in 1770— seemingly a typical year for him—Charlton sold 20 brown dress queue wigs, three grizzle bobs, one each of three other styles, made curls or dressed ladies' hair on 28 occasions, and had 42 annual customers for shaving and dressing. During the court or Assembly sessions many additional patrons demanded these last services. All of his 1770 business should have brought Charlton well over £300 in 1771, when most payments would have been made. Actually he received roughly £260 in that year, with the balance probably dribbling in over the next decade—or in some cases never paid.

The difficulties of debt collection were among the reasons why so many colonial Virginia craftsmen sought to augment their income by branching into some other activity. Williamsburg wigmakers favored innkeeping as their second occupation. No fewer than five operated ordinaries or provided lodgings, and one of them, Robert Lyon, moved on to become a merchant. David Cunningham served as the town constable for several years, and Alexander Finnie, of

*A facsimile of Andrew Anderson's bill to Colonel Thomas Jones, then of Williamsburg, for services to various members of the latter's household, apparently including servants, during 1741, 1742, and 1743. Note that there are more entries for pulling teeth and bleeding the sick than for making and dressing wigs. (Reproduced by permission from the Jones Family Papers, Library of Congress.)*

course, left the wig trade entirely to become host of the Raleigh Tavern.

In addition to wigmaking, shaving, and hairdressing, Andrew Anderson practiced dentistry and phlebotomy (bleeding). But these were traditional phases of the barbering craft, not extra occupations—albeit only Anderson among Williamsburg barbers practiced them so far as we know.

Charlton at one time took a flier in real estate along with John Stretch, bookbinder and bookkeeper in William Hunter's printing office. The partners bought the playhouse and lot (about where Mrs. Campbell's Tavern now stands) from Lewis Hallam, proprietor of the Company of Comedians recently from London. The evidence is inconclusive, but suggests that the venture was not a glittering success.

From time to time Charlton recorded the sale of such items as a "Ferkin of butter," a gross of bottles (apparently empty), "eight pounds Chooklate," stockings, "five Hundred Limes," a piece of linen, three dozen strong beer, one "cheas," and part of a lottery ticket. However intriguing these entries may be, they are too infrequent and irregular to support a conclusion that the barber was running a retail store on the side. When so much business was done by barter, any craftsman might have incongruous articles to sell.

Like the silversmith James Geddy, Jr., and other craftsmen of Williamsburg, Charlton once served on the city's common council. This position carried no compensation, but election to it showed that a man's neighbors trusted and respected him.

The tradition of the humble artisan whose industry and integrity earned him the esteem of his fellow citizens ran strong in colonial America. Unfortunately for the wigmakers, however, no bulwark could withstand the ebb tide of fashion. George Lafong, whose Williamsburg wig shop rivaled Charlton's in the early 1770s, ended as a beggar in

1796. Someone, it seems, must pay the price for every forward step in the march of progress. Were it not so, all of us might still be wearing wigs today.

---

## *THE BARBERS AND WIGMAKERS OF WILLIAMSBURG*

*Andrew Anderson*—Apprenticed for seven years to John Peter Wagnon of Williamsburg in 1731. After only five years became his own master and bought Wagnon's shop next to the Raleigh Tavern. The only Williamsburg barber known to have practiced dentistry and phlebotomy. Frequently in court as witness, plaintiff, or defendant in suits over property, debts, etc. Sold out to William Peake, Yorktown barber and wigmaker, and was preparing to leave for England when he died suddenly in 1752.

*Stephen Besouth*—Died April 3, 1726, leaving an estate appraised at £40 12s. 1d. and consisting almost solely of articles suitable to barbering and wigmaking.

*Daniel Blouett*—Arrived in Virginia in 1700 as a Huguenot refugee. Bought a lot in Williamsburg in 1713, the deed identifying him as a "Peruke-Maker." Died in 1720. His name was variously spelled (or misspelled) in different records: Blouet, Bluet, Bleuet, Blewitt, Blewit, Blewet, Blouett, and Blouette.

*John Borton*—The *Virginia Gazette* of March 3, 1768, published a list of letters in the post office waiting to be claimed by their addressees. One was for "John Borton, perukemaker, Williamsburg." Nothing more is known of him.

*Simon Brazier*—A partner of Anthony Geohegan, Williamsburg barber and wigmaker, from April to about November 1768.

*John Bryan*—A partner of Alexander Maitland in the wigmaking craft in 1752 and later sole proprietor of a shop on Williamsburg's main street. Possibly moved away from the town in 1756.

*Edward Charlton*—In 1752, soon after arriving from London, became a partner of Richard Gamble in the latter's shop next door to the Raleigh Tavern. Continued the business after Gamble's death and was the town's foremost wigmaker until the Revolution. Died sometime between 1783 and 1792.

*Richard Charlton*—Presumably related to Edward. Probably was not himself a barber or wigmaker, but was briefly an inactive partner of James Nichols, Williamsburg wigmaker, and on occasion purveyed wigs to customers of his well-patronized tavern.

*David Cunningham*—In addition to barbering and wigmaking, operated an ordinary (inn) at his house near the Capitol and for several years served as constable of Williamsburg. Died in 1720.

*James Currie*—Took over in 1752 the former shop of Andrew Anderson in partnership with William Peake of Yorktown. Later moved across the street to his own shop. Ordered in 1759 to pay the support of "Mary Seveney's Bastard Child." May have left town thereafter, as his shop and the lot it stood on were sold in 1761.

*William Davenport*—An inventoried appraisal of his estate in 1770 listed a number of items used by barbers and wigmakers.

*Mr. Davidson*—The register of Bruton Parish Church in Williamsburg records the death on October 1, 1749, of "Mr. Davidson—the Barber." Nothing more is known of him.

*William Duncan*—Was an indentured servant in 1753 of Robert Lyon, Williamsburg wigmaker. Died two years later, leaving an estate appraised by three other wigmakers at £28 and consisting mostly of wigmaking articles and supplies.

*Alexander Finnie*—Seemingly successful as wigmaker, tavernkeeper, and property-owner. Advertised in 1745 for two or three journeymen, luring one from Andrew Anderson, and imported more the next year. Acquired the Raleigh Tavern in 1749 and the new (second) theater in 1751, actively managing the former until he sold both properties in 1752. At his death in 1769 also owned Porto Bello plantation outside Williamsburg.

*Richard Gamble*—From 1743 onward regularly cited in court records for failing to attend church and to pay debts. In 1752 took Edward Charlton into partnership to run his shop next to the Raleigh. Died in 1755 leaving no known family or real property and only £14 worth of barbering and wigmaking articles.

*Anthony Geohegan*—Opened shop next door to Mrs. Vobe's tavern across from the Raleigh in 1768. Took Simon Brazier briefly into partnership the same year. Moved to Richmond sometime between 1770 and 1775, having in the meantime married Martha Lavia, Williamsburg widow.

*William Godfrey*—Announced in 1766 that he had opened shop between the Raleigh Tavern and the Capitol. Nothing more is known of his wigmaking activities, but he figured in several court cases during the following seven years.

*Thomas Hewitt*—Was an indentured servant of Robert Lyon in 1753 and may have had his own shop in Williamsburg before moving to Annapolis about 1762.

*Cuthbert Hubbard*—In 1771 advertised that he was still carrying on his wigmaking business in addition to offering lodgings. Died in 1779. His will mentioned only teenth century the golden age of the barber had begun.

For most of the seventeenth and eighteenth centuries in Europe an inordinate emphasis on appearance led to excesses of fashion in both costume and hairdress. Men followed the vagaries of high fashion as faithfully as women, and vied with each other in wearing long curls of their own or somebody else's hair.

The wearing of wigs, at least for special purposes, was of ancient origin. Wigs have been found on Egyptian mummies; Greek actors wore wigs on stage; fashionable ladies of Rome and Carthage were much addicted to false hair—especially golden locks from Teuton heads. But the widespread wearing of perukes as an everyday article of costume is generally held to date from 1624, when Louis XIII adopted the usage.

Here it needs to be said, perhaps, that "wig" and "peruke" are not different styles but different forms of the same word. The French *perruque*, spelled *peruke* in England and the colonies, had gone through an earlier series of English transformations: from *perwyke* to *perewyk* to *periwig*, and then by abbreviation to *wig*.

Although Louis XIV disdained wigs until his abundant natural hair began to fall out, the fashion flourished at his court and was brought over to England by the restored Charles II, who began in 1663 to affect a large black wig. Charles may have been the first English king to adopt the custom, but it is said that Elizabeth I owned some 80 auburn, orange, and gold wigs to cover her thinning hair.

Just as Louis XIII's courtiers hastened to don wigs as soon as their monarch did, so aspiring ladies and gentlemen of Restoration England emulated their king. Samuel Pepys recorded that his wife first acquired "a pair of peruques of hair, as the fashion now is for ladies to wear; which are pretty, and are of my wife's own hair, or else I should not endure them." Then, after great hesitation, he bought a "periwigg" for himself and had his hair cut off and made into another.

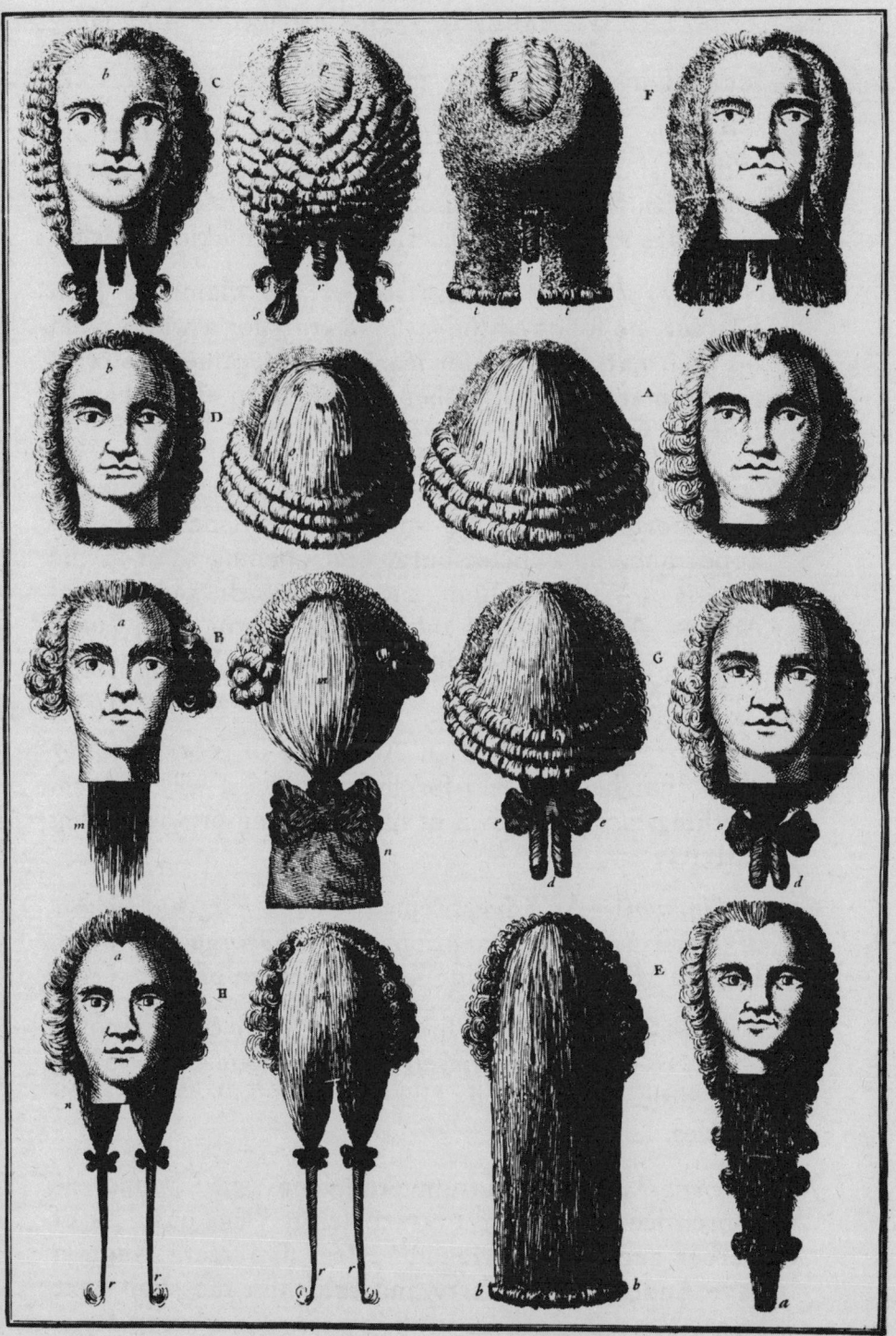

*This page from François-Alexandre-Pierre de Garsault's* The Art of the Wigmaker, *with illustrations similar to those of Diderot's* Encyclopedia, *shows the following styles: (by letter, not in the usual order): (A) bonnet or short wig; (B) bag wig; (C) knotted wig; (D) clerical wig; (E) natural wig; (F) square wig; (G) brigadier wig; and (H) double pigtail wig.*

for rent in 1779, and by 1784 was located in Norfolk.

*Jean Pasteur*—A Huguenot refugee, who had settled in Williamsburg by 1703. Appeared in court in the usual roles with the usual frequency. Died in 1741, leaving a moderate amount of barbering and wigmaking articles.

*[John] James Pasteur*—Eldest son of the wigmaker Jean Pasteur, he followed his father's craft for a while, then his own natural bent for learning. Became master of a grammar school and then an Anglican clergyman in Norfolk County.

*William Peake*—A Yorktown barber, wigmaker, and dealer in imported wigmaking supplies who made a brief appearance in Williamsburg, first opening shop in the tavern of William Dunn, then buying the old shop of Andrew Anderson and taking into partnership James Currie. Currie seems to have run the Williamsburg end of the combine while Peake returned to Yorktown.

*Edward Perry*—The Guardian Accounts of York County show that he was paid for shaving and a wig in 1748. Nothing more is known of his barbering or wigmaking activity.

*George Simmons*—An advertisement in the *Virginia Gazette* of April 14, 1774, mentions "Mr. George Simmons, Peruke Maker." Nothing more is known of him.

*Robert Tennoch*—His name first appeared in court records of 1722. Described himself as "Perukemaker" in his will, probated in 1726. His estate included barbering articles.

*John Peter Wagnon*—Andrew Anderson was bound as apprentice to him in 1731 to learn "the business of Barber and Peruke Maker." After five years Wagnon gave Anderson his liberty and sold him the shop next to the Raleigh Tavern.

*Alexander Wiley*—Became a partner of George Lafong in 1775 and continued so at least until 1777, the last known appearance of his name.

## SUGGESTIONS FOR FURTHER READING

Janet Arnold, *Perukes & Periwigs.* London: Her Majesty's Stationery Office, 1970.

Anne Buck, *Dress in Eighteenth-Century England.* London: B. T. Batsford, Ltd., 1979.

Diana de Marly, *Fashion for Men: An Illustrated History.* London: B. T. Batsford, Ltd., 1985.

Gail Durbin, *Wig, Hairdressing and Shaving Bygones.* Aylesbury, England: Shire Publications Ltd., 1984.

François Alexandre Pierre de Garsault, *Art of the Wigmaker: Comprising the Shaping of the Beard; The Cutting of Hair; The Construction of Wigs for Ladies & Gentlemen; The Renovation of Wigs and the Bath and Hot Room Proprietor.* Translation of *Art du Perruquier* (Paris, 1767), ed. J. Stevens-Cox. London: Hairdressers' Registration Council, 1961.

Maria Jedding-Gesterling, ed., *Hairstyles: A Cultural History of Fashions in Hair from Antiquity up to the Present Day.* Hamburg, Germany: Hans Schwarzkopf GmbH, 1988.

Bernard Lens, *The Exact Dress of the Head.* London: The Costume Society, 1970.

Marcia Pointon, *Hanging the Head.* New Haven, Conn.: Yale University Press, 1993.

James Stevens-Cox, *Illustrated Dictionary of Hairdressing &*
     *Wigmaking: Containing Words, Terms and Phrases (Current*
     *and Obsolete), Dialectal, Foreign, and Technical, Used in Brit-*
     *ain and America.* London: Batsford Academic and Educa-
     tional, 1984.

C. Willet and Phyllis Cunnington, *Handbook of English Costume*
     *in the Eighteenth Century.* Rev. ed. Boston: Plays, Inc., 1972.

*The Wigmaker in Eighteenth-Century Williamsburg* is based
largely on an unpublished monograph by Thomas K. Bul-
lock and Maurice B. Tonkin, Jr., formerly of the Colonial
Williamsburg research staff, assisted by Raymond R.
Townsend, former researcher in crafts. It was first published
in 1959 and previously reprinted in 1965, 1968, 1971, 1979,
1987, 1990, 1996, and 1998.

ISBN 0-910412-22-7

90000

9 780910 412223